richmond park

a year in the life of richmond park joanna jackson

FRANCES LINCOLN

a year in the life of richmond park joanna jackson

For my wonderful mother whose unwavering support, *joie de vivre* and incredible optimism will always be an inspiration to me.

Many thanks to: Simon Richards, the Park Superintendent, who very kindly read and checked the text of this book. To Nigel Reeve, the Park Ecologist, who helped me with the identification of some of the more obscure creatures and plants. To Liz Attenborough for encouraging me and for giving me the benefit of her enormous experience in publishing. To my husband, whose computer skills helped produce the initial draft of the book. And to my friend Rosemary for taking me on a Charlie Waite landscape photography course many years ago.

Frances Lincoln Limited
4 Torriano Mews
Torriano Avenue
London NW5 2RZ

A Year in the Life of Richmond Park
Copyright © Frances Lincoln Limited 2003

Text and photographs copyright © Joanna Jackson

First Frances Lincoln edition 2003

Joanna Jackson has asserted her moral right to be identified as Author of this Work in accordance with the Copyright, Designs and Patents Act 1988.

British Library cataloguing-in-publication data
A catalogue record for this book is available from
the British Library

ISBN 0-7112-2218-5

Printed in China

contents

richmond park: a brief history

'The King [Charles], who was excessively affected to hunting, and the sports of the field, had a great desire to make a great Park for red, as well as fallow deer, between Richmond and Hampton Court,' wrote Edward Hyde, Earl of Clarendon, in his *History of the Rebellion and the Civil Wars of England Begun in the Year 1641*. Although he had land at James I's New Park as well as at Hampton Court, Charles coveted an area of gravel uplands – the area now covered by Richmond Park – which would provide good hunting country. The common land available was irregular in shape, so as well as enclosing it the King decided to purchase adjoining privately owned land to make a park of a more suitable size and shape. Despite generous financial offers from the Crown, most of the landowners were very unwilling to hand over their property, which in many cases had been in their families for generations, and by 1635 only 5 acres/2 hectares of land had been bought. However, Charles, who was used to riding roughshod over people to get what he wanted, had already started work on building a high brick wall that was eventually to surround the whole park to his specifications, regardless of whether the private owners gave consent. The wall made him very unpopular, but although his advisors tried to persuade him against building it, with characteristic arrogance he persisted. By 1637 the enclosure was complete and Charles had created a deer park of 2,500 acres/1011 hectares.

On Charles's death in 1649 the Commonwealth government gave the park to the City of London in thanks for support in the Civil War but the Corporation of London restored it to the monarchy in 1660 when Charles II was restored to the throne.

The issue of access

The people had always had free access to the park, for walking and collecting firewood. Though in 1673 the gates were locked to keep out livestock, ladderstiles were put up around the wall to provide access for the local people. It was considered good entertainment to watch royalty hunting for deer and turkey and considerable crowds would congregate. By 1735 so many people were coming

that anxiety arose that they were 'not only troublesome but very dangerous'. George II's consort, Queen Caroline, issued a notice saying that only people with a hunting ticket, to be obtained from the Park Ranger, could enter the park. Further restrictions followed: tickets for carriages became necessary, authorized keyholders had to go to the lodges to enter the park and the locks on the gates were changed to prevent people who had obtained keys illegally from entering. In 1751, George II's youngest daughter, Princess Amelia, became Park Ranger and she attempted to make the area completely private. While beating the bounds, a parish party found their usual access point, a ladderstile into the park, mysteriously missing. The party either broke down part of the wall or climbed over a broken section. When the Princess got wind of this, she closed the park to everyone except her own personal guests.

In 1755, John Lewis, a local brewer, took a case of pedestrian right of way to the Kingston Assizes. It was three years before his case was heard, but eventually he won back pedestrian access to the park for everyone. This was not the end of the story, though: the ladders that were put up had rungs that were so far apart that the old and the very young could not use them, and it was necessary to go back to court. Again Lewis won his case and ladders that were easier to climb were provided. Partly as a result of the vast expenses he incurred on these lawsuits (as well as of the flooding of his brewery when the Thames overflowed at Petersham), later in life John Lewis fell into great poverty. As a sign of their appreciation of his work for the park the residents of Richmond contributed to provide a small annuity for him in his old age.

The issue of the right of access to the park continues to cause unrest among local people today, when arguments rage about the shutting of some gates to prevent the park from overuse by cars.

A place for public pleasure

The park gradually ceased to be used as a hunting ground and by the end of the eighteenth century it had become instead a place to promenade. The Deputy Ranger of that time, Viscount Sidmouth, was passionate about trees and was responsible for much planting of woodland.

The next big change occurred in the early twentieth century, when Edward VII decided to develop the park as a public amenity. Areas were laid out for golf courses and football and cricket pitches and most of the previously fenced woods were opened to the public.

Wartime changes

The two world wars of the twentieth century provided an enormous upheaval to life in the park. During both wars much of the park was put to pasture, and sheep and cattle were to be seen in place of the deer, whose numbers were greatly reduced by culls to provide venison to supplement the dwindling meat supplies. Oats and potatoes were grown by East Sheen Gate. Garden allotments administered by Richmond Borough Council were sited in the north-west corner of the park. Military camps and hospitals were built in the park, and there were continual military manoeuvres.

During the 1914–18 war a large military encampment was established where the golf courses are now, and a war hospital was built for the use of the South African Army between Conduit Wood and Bishop's Lodge. Cambrian Gate was erected specifically to serve this unit. The hospital was eventually demolished in 1925.

During the war of 1939–45 over a quarter of the park was put under cultivation or used as grazing land. A large military encampment of semi-permanent buildings was built at Kingston Gate to house the East Surrey Regiment.

The Pen Ponds were drained and camouflaged to prevent the Luftwaffe using them as a navigational aid. Anti-aircraft gun batteries were placed strategically around the park to attack enemy aircraft during the London Blitz. A 'sterilizing pit' was built between Ham Cross and the Isabella Plantation. This was used for bleeding explosives from unexploded enemy bombs.

In 1948, the army camp was used as a rather Spartan Olympic village for the London games and in 1956 as temporary housing for service families evacuated from the Suez Canal zone. The buildings were demolished in 1965.

The park today

Today hardly any sign remains of the turmoil of the war years. Richmond Park is again a wonderful space for public enjoyment. There is a large café in the well-appointed Pembroke Lodge and many of the car parks now have mobile cafeterias providing welcome sustenance at the end of a walk. Rugby and polo are still played, kite flying is very popular and there is a model aircraft club that has a special area set aside for its use. Fishermen still make use of Pen Ponds. A recently built cycle path runs around the perimeter and bicycles can be hired from the car park near Roehampton Gate. And of course there are any number of walks to be enjoyed.

A red deer stag, antlers covered in snow, awaits better weather.

the deer

There are about 650 deer in the park: 375 fallow deer and 275 red deer. The male red deer is called a stag and the female a hind; the fallow deer male is a buck and the female a doe. The red deer are the larger animals, with the stags standing 40–48 inches/100–122 cm at the shoulder. In the winter the coat is dark brown, coarse outer hair covering a fine inner one. The individual hairs are hollow, providing good insulation in cold weather.

The fallow deer, the smaller of the two types, come in three different colourings. The black, who have dark coats with no lighter coloured spots; the menil, the commonest, which have pale coats with distinctive spots in summer, with a few retained in the winter; and the white, whose coat is pure white with no coloured spots. The word 'fallow' derives from the Anglo-Saxon 'fealewe', referring to the yellowish brown colour of the menil doe's coat in summer.

The fallow deer are the more nervous of the two. They defend themselves by forming a bunch. When alarmed they can move quickly with a 'pronking' gait (all four feet moving together). The decision to break and run is made by the lead doe, who is followed by the remaining does and fawns backed up by the bucks.

The red deer, though for most of the year passive when not harrassed, are far more likely to stand their ground. The hinds are particularly aggressive when they have young and often chase people away from the area where their calves are hiding. The males become aggressive in the rut in the autumn, when hormones, lack of sleep and food, and a general increase in tension make them more unpredictable and agitated than normal. It is sensible to stay away from them then and leave them in peace and allow deer life to go on without the interference of people. In the interests of the deer it is vital that dogs are always kept under control when in their vicinity. The deer become very stressed when they are chased by dogs and if they turn on the dogs can injure or even kill them.

The females give birth in June and July. Both fallow and red deer usually have only one offspring. Immediately after the birth the young are left hidden in the undergrowth. They are too weak to follow the herd so the mothers feed close by, keeping an eye on their young.

As winter sets in, the search for food becomes more difficult. At this time the deer can become quite destructive to the tree population, in particular stripping bark. This is the reason for the timber tree guards in the park – to protect the vulnerable young trees. Deer can scrape away snow to get at the grass beneath but find several days of hard frost more difficult to cope with. From November to March the deer in the park are given supplementary feeds of maize, hay and special deer pellets. They are fed at night at traditional stands. As the deer gather to eat, the gamekeepers who look after them monitor their condition and adjust their feeding regime accordingly. This is also a time to select weak and old animals to be culled. They are noted and culled in November and again in February. The deer have no natural predators and without the cull the herd would grow beyond the carrying capacity of the park. This would result in their starvation and the devastation of their habitat. The cull ensures a healthy herd with the correct balance of ages and sexes that the park's grazing can support.

LEFT: A bird finds a perching place on the back of a red deer, as the deer and its calf stare intently at the photographer.

RIGHT, ABOVE: A stag party, escaping the heat of the summer, takes refuge in the shade.

RIGHT, BELOW : A fallow deer suckles its young fawn.

winter

The months of December, January and February can be awful: days of constant cloud cover when you forget what the sun looks like, days of pouring rain with the ground underfoot getting soggier and soggier. But they can also be beautiful, with hoarfrosts and, in an exceptional year, magical snowfalls. The light, being low, casts long, interesting shadows, and because the days are short it is possible to experience wonderful sunrises without having to get up ridiculously early.

The Pen Ponds fill up with migratory wildfowl seeking refuge from colder climes. In February woodpeckers can be heard in most of the copses in the park. Their characteristic drumming noise is created by the bird rapidly banging its beak on a resonant surface such as a dead branch.

With the bracken having died back, fox, badger and rabbit holes are visible, and on the leafless trees holes may be easily seen. These holes may be natural or made by woodpeckers in past years. The chances are that if there is a nice hole it will be used by somebody as a nest site. If you note the signs now, when you come back later in the year it will be easier to spot any activity at these sites.

OPPOSITE: Frosted trees on a beautiful winter's morning.

BELOW: A copse of trees by the rugby pitches provides shelter for the fallow deer on a freezing day.

OVERLEAF: One of the oldest, most perfect oaks in the park stands in splendid isolation near Barn Wood.

winter ponds and migration

There are twenty-three ponds in the park, the largest being the Pen Ponds in the centre. The original Pen Pond is now known as Leg of Mutton Pond. It is located about 218 yards/200 metres west of the new Pen Ponds. These new Pen Ponds are assumed to have been made as a result of the excavation of gravel for use in the local construction industry. There is a record of 8,000 loads of gravel being removed between 1677 and 1683. In the eighteenth century Princess Amelia, when Park Ranger, converted the gravel pits into ornamental ponds. There is a romantic notion that the ponds were named after the female swans or 'pens' that resided there, but the name is more probably to do with proximity to a deer pen.

The Pen Ponds have resident populations of coots, moorhens, pochards, swans, Canada geese and great crested grebes. In the winter they provide a home to many birds that are heading south for the cold months, seeking shelter and less harsh climates. Regular migratory visitors are wigeon, gadwall and shoveller.

Wigeon are small birds with short beaks and short legs. They have a very distinctive call – 'whee-oo' – that echoes across the cold water. When the sunlight catches a wigeon's forehead, the top shines with a golden hue. There is no known breeding of wigeon south of Yorkshire, and they visit for only a couple of months.

The gadwall is rather dull in appearance: its plumage is a mixture of silver, black and brown and it has a black bottom and beak.

At first glance the shoveller duck can easily be mistaken for a mallard: it has a similar green head and patches of brown and white. The obvious difference is the long broad bill that it uses to sieve water, looking for food. It is also a bigger and heavier bird than a mallard.

In January 2002 a bittern was sighted many times at the ponds as well as at the nearby Wetlands Trust in Barnes. Being the first bittern to be sighted in London for over a hundred years, it attracted much media attention.

The reed bed at the back of the upper Pen Pond has been enclosed to keep out deer, whose trampling and grazing has resulted in deterioration of this important habitat. Work has started on cutting back encroaching rhododendrons to encourage the regeneration of adjacent reed fern.

TOP: Gulls and a solitary coot perch on the ice. They stand on one leg and tuck their beaks in their wings to conserve body heat.

BOTTOM: Unmelted snowflakes on the frozen upper Pen Pond.

LEFT: The upper Pen Pond, full of gulls, which head inland in bad weather.

isabella plantation in winter

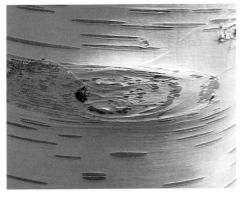

Though the Isabella Plantation is best known for its magnificent display of rhododendrons and azaleas in spring, it is a wonderfully serene place to visit at any other time of year, when it is much less crowded.

During the winter months of December, January and February there are many interesting specimen trees and shrubs with coloured, textured bark. In the new Bog Garden, yellow and red-stemmed dogwoods are planted by a weeping willow. Pollarded willows on the banks of Peg's Pond have amber and red stems. Three Himalayan birches with striking white stems are on the lawn by Thompson's Pond. To the north-east of Thompson's Pond is a Tibetan cherry, which has mahogany red bark. In the acer glade there are several 'snake bark' acers.

A favourite shrub in winter is the Chinese witch hazel to be found at the entrance gate to the plantation, which can be reached from the main Broomfield Hill car park. As you enter the plantation, the witch hazel's amazing heady perfume fills the air and makes you want to stand still and just take it in.

The Heather Garden by Peg's Pond is in bloom throughout the winter.

In February there are early rhododendrons and camellias to be found dotted around. In a usually overcast and gloomy season it is always a nice feeling to walk round a corner and be confronted by an unexpected flash of colour.

The plantation provides a rich and varied habitat for birds and animals. The deer are not allowed into the area, because of the damage they would cause, but all other animals are free to come and go as they please. Many badgers, foxes, rabbits and squirrels make their home there. There are pinioned ducks, all native species, present year round on Peg's Pond, and wild birds also visit. Many small birds are inhabitants but predatory sparrowhawks hide in the trees waiting for an opportunity to ambush them. A pile of feathers lying on the path is a sign that a sparrowhawk has had a meal recently.

OPPOSITE, TOP: The red stems of dogwood show up well against the snow in the Isabella Plantation Bog Garden.

OPPOSITE, BOTTOM LEFT: Tibetan cherry bark.

OPPOSITE, BOTTOM RIGHT: Himalayan birch bark.

BELOW: Snow hangs on the bare trees by a frozen Thompson's Pond in the Isabella Plantation.

hibernation

When the food supply begins to diminish, the weather begins to get colder and more hostile, and many birds migrate to warmer, more hospitable climes, what do the mammals and reptiles do? Many creatures cope with the most unpleasant months of the year by hibernating: when the going gets tough they retreat to a safe hiding place and enter a sleep-like state. This inactivity can be triggered by a fall of temperature, a lack of food or a change in the length of day. Before hibernating, animals put on weight, building up reserves of body fat to keep them going during their deep sleep. While asleep, an animal's body temperature falls almost to that of its surroundings and its breathing, heart rate and digestion slow down so that its metabolic rate is very low and makes few demands of its system.

Hedgehogs are very deep hibernators and may at times stop breathing for up to an hour before needing air again. They wake up in March and are ready to breed by April. However, interestingly, there are no hedgehogs to be found in the park. This is because of the park's large badger population – badgers prey on hedgehogs.

Bats also hibernate, but their hibernation is not so deep. They often wake on warmer days. It is during winter that mating occurs, although fertilization is delayed until April. In the park bats may be found hibernating in holes in the trees.

Amphibians and reptiles are cold-blooded, so when environmental temperatures drop they enter a state of torpor, which enables them to maintain their body temperature. Frogs find sheltered places on land or go to the muddy bottoms of ponds. Toads stay under logs or stones, often in large groups not too far from their breeding grounds. Newts also hibernate on land.

OPPOSITE: Shafts of light diffused through the fog in the trees by Pembroke Lodge.

LEFT, ABOVE: A heron spookily lurks in the fog in Beverley Brook.

LEFT, BELOW: The sun breaks through clouds over the upper Pen Pond.

A stark oak tree stands alone on the rugby grounds.

white lodge

White Lodge was built in the Palladian style in 1727, commissioned by George II from the Earl of Pembroke and Roger Morris; these two men were also responsible for Marble Hill House in Twickenham.

From 1801 George III commissioned various architects to enlarge White Lodge. One of these was James Wyatt, a Gothic Revivalist whose restorations of medieval cathedrals had earned him the nickname 'the Destroyer'. He duly destroyed the Palladian splendour of White Lodge. The lodge was subsequently added to and it is today a hotchpotch of architectural styles.

George III used White Lodge as a hunting box but he never lived there, and on Henry Addington's appointment as prime minister he gave it to him to live in. Addington stayed on in White Lodge after his resignation, when he became Viscount Sidmouth. He took over the management of the park and distinguished himself as a great park manager. The extensive tree planting for which he was responsible includes Sidmouth Wood.

The best view of White Lodge is from Queen's Ride, a magnificent tree-lined avenue that was made through existing woodland so that Queen Caroline, George II's consort, could reach White Lodge. She would enter the park at Queen's Gate (now Bog Gate), which had been specifically cut through the wall for her, and travel down the avenue to her favourite residence.

It is said that it was while dining at White Lodge Nelson came up with his strategic battle plan to defeat the French at Trafalgar.

Today White Lodge is the home of the Royal Ballet School.

Two stags test their strength
against each other in front of
White Lodge.

Sunrise over Pen Ponds.

Sunrise over the riding circle.

ABOVE: Beverley Brook by
Roehampton Gate.

LEFT: Early morning at the pond
near the Sawpit Plantation.

Trees near Conduit Wood,
covered by a hoarfrost.

Frosted grasses.

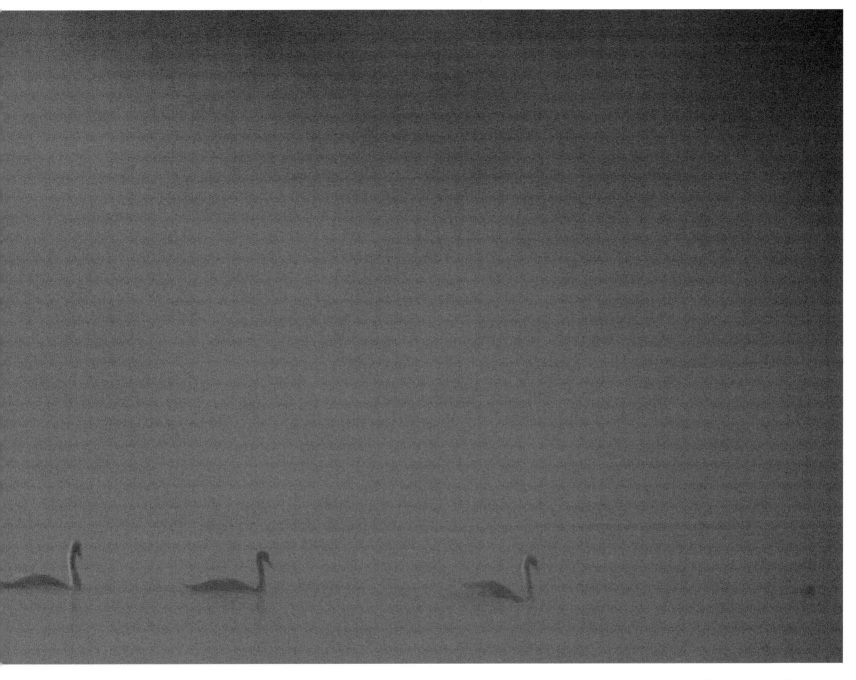

Five swans glide silently across
the upper Pen Pond in fog.

LEFT: The skeleton of a tree by Two Storm Wood.

RIGHT, ABOVE: Mist in the valley by Duchess Wood.

RIGHT, BELOW: Reflections of trees in the pond near White Ash Lodge.

spring

Spring brings great changes to the grassland, as with the warmth and light of longer days the winter's washed-out shades are replaced by the vibrant colours of wild flowers and fresh grass.

This is the best time of year to hear birds sing. The cuckoo arrives in May and can usually be heard around the Isabella Plantation. Skylarks, often not visible because they fly so high, are audible by the riding circle and the flat areas near Pen Ponds.

The word 'spring' comes from the woodland. It originally referred to the sprays of fresh green shoots that appear as the days lengthen. To a woodsman the reference was specifically to the new shoots sprouting from the hazel stumps that had been cut the previous autumn.

In the woods, trees are in flower. Trees must flower, be pollinated and set seed in order to produce a new generation. Most woodland trees are wind pollinated, so they don't need to waste energy producing showy flowers, and many native species have insignificant green blossoms. Hay fever sufferers are certainly aware of their flowers, however. The most potent pollen in the early spring comes from alder, elm, hazel and poplar trees. In late spring and early summer, pollen from birch and oak add to hay fever misery.

In the Isabella Plantation the azaleas and rhododendrons are at their best and bluebells carpet the ground. Ferns begin to unfurl from under the surface of the soil.

Frogs and toads set out to make and lay their spawn in the pond where they were born. Toads will travel up to a mile, often following routes their ancestors used before roads were built, and many are killed crossing roads. In the park they may be seen trying to cross the road to get to Ham Pond. Frogs are less choosy, and may spawn in the first pond they come across.

Once at their spawning ponds, frogs and toads mate and deposit masses of jelly-like spawn. When the frogs get to the pond, there is often a mating frenzy, when clusters of frogs can be seen clinging together. By the end of March most of the smaller ponds in the park and many of the streams have quantities of spawn in them. Frog spawn is a mass of clear round balls of jelly; toad spawn is laid in strings 3–6 feet/1–2 metres long, often twisted round weed to anchor it.

The amount of spawn in the park has dropped off dramatically in recent years and the public are urged not to collect it but to leave it where it is, in an effort to increase the numbers of the park's amphibians.

isabella plantation in spring

In May the Isabella Plantation is at its most colourful. A walk through the centre of the enclosed woodland garden takes you past the vivid pink, scarlet and purple flowers of the azaleas. The impact of the colour scheme is almost overwhelming. To the left and right of Broomfield Hill Gate, trails following the perimeter fence take you on an altogether different experience through wild bluebell patches and highly perfumed yellow and orange azaleas – a more subtle stroll but equally beautiful. The Bog Garden is full of gunnera (a giant plant from the rhubarb family), marsh marigolds and unfurling new fern leaves which resemble the ornate twirls that adorn the end of banisters. The grass area by Thompson's Pond blooms towards the end of May, when the rhododendron centrepiece is at its best.

The plantation was originally known as Isabella Slade. 'Isabell' means 'dingy yellow', possibly referring to the yellow clay topsoil found in the area. The word 'slade' described a shallow valley.

The area was first enclosed in 1831. Oak, beech and sweet chestnut trees were planted then. There are many much older oaks within the plantation, however, including one thought to have been present before the original enclosure of the park in 1637. When the famous plant collector Ernest Wilson introduced many different azaleas from Japan into Britain in 1920, the plantation became home to the National Collection of Kurume azaleas. All known examples from this collection are planted here, as well as other plants Wilson introduced to this country. Many are to be found in and around Wilson's Glade.

However, the plantation was not really developed until the late 1940s, when it was transformed from a simple streamside walk to a spectacular woodland garden with glades, streams, ponds, heather and bog gardens. This reinvention of the area was down to the drive and vision of George Thompson, the Park Superintendent at the time, and his head gardener, Wally Miller. It was opened as the Woodland Garden in 1953.

It is possible to make a self-guided tour of the area. The tour is arranged so that interesting specimens can be viewed. Numbers on wooden stakes identify these special plants and trees near them. A booklet giving details about the walk and the labelled plants is available from Holly Lodge.

FAR LEFT: Bluebells.

LEFT: A perfect dandelion seed head.

OPPOSITE: The wilder part of the Isabella Plantation, with bluebells and orange and yellow perfumed azaleas competing for attention.

ABOVE: Marsh marigolds and
mallards in the Bog Garden
in the Isabella Plantation.

LEFT: A sunlit stream in the
Isabella Plantation.

OPPOSITE, ABOVE: The more cultivated and showy area of the Isabella Plantation, with rhododendrons and azaleas in their full glory.

OPPOSITE, BELOW LEFT: Daffodils with a bumblebee after some pollen.

OPPOSITE, BELOW RIGHT: A beautiful azalea flower.

RIGHT: Still Pond, surrounded by vibrantly coloured azaleas that are reflected in the water.

hawthorn and gorse regeneration

In the north-west corner of the park a programme to regenerate the hawthorn and gorse has begun. Areas of gorse and small saplings of hawthorn have been fenced in. The fencing is necessary to protect the new growth from the grazing deer.

Gorse is a dense, prickly evergreen shrub. One saying goes, 'When the gorse is out of bloom, kissing is out of fashion'; according to another, 'While the gorse is in flower, Britain will never be conquered.' Nobody need be alarmed, though, for gorse is in bloom almost all year round, with its most prolific flowering in spring and summer. The gorse in the park is an important site for the small birds that love to rest in it, the vicious thorns providing good protection against predators. It is hoped that the rare Dartford warbler might be tempted back to the park by the gorse.

The hawthorn tree is fast-growing and sturdy, providing an almost impenetrable barrier if planted alongside others as a hedge. Landowners used to plant it as a surrounding hedge to their estates, where it provided food and protection for wildlife. With the mechanization of farming, many such natural barriers have been replaced by electric fences, so removing one of nature's friends.

Hawthorn, sometimes called may, is linked to pagan and medieval rites for greeting the advent of summer. This association probably arose because hawthorn blossoms in mid-May – around May Day in the unreformed Christian calendar. In country areas, destruction of hawthorn was believed to invite peril and to bring blossom indoors was to court disaster.

The berries hawthorn produces in the autumn provide a valuable food source for many birds, including winter visitors such as fieldfare and redwing.

RIGHT: Gorse in flower.

OPPOSITE: As ferns emerge from the ground, they unfurl majestically.

OVERLEAF: Early morning mist over Beverley Brook.

antlers of the red deer

March is the month in which the oldest stags in the red deer herd cast their antlers. The younger members of the group will carry theirs until the end of April.

Permanent bony pedicles upon the skull become visible in the male calf at about his first Christmas and it is upon these pedicles that the antlers grow each year, after last year's antlers have been shed. The individual pattern of antlers for each deer is replicated annually, with a few additions. During the first year the antlers are only single spikes. Every year the antlers become grander, with more and more spikes. This enables the male deer to establish their place within the hierarchy of the herd without having to resort to fights, which may end in injury.

The renewal of the antlers strains the deer's metabolism, demanding calcium and phosphorus, and in areas of mineral deficiency antlers are less ornate. In Richmond Park the deer are well fed, and their antlers grow very large and elaborate.

While the antlers are growing, they are covered by a hairy skin called velvet. Blood vessels in the velvet supply food and oxygen to the growing bone. When the velvet is shed the antlers die, although they remain on the deer's head until the next spring. You cannot tell the age of a deer exactly by the number of 'tines', or points, on a pair of antlers but you can tell whether he is old or young – the more points, the older the stag.

ABOVE: A healthy young stag with his antlers coated in velvet.

OPPOSITE: A red deer starting new buds for antlers.

pembroke lodge

Today Pembroke Lodge and its gardens are open to the public. There is a cafeteria and the Russell Rooms provide indoor seating where one can enjoy afternoon tea after a stroll through the park. In the summer, bands play jazz at Sunday lunchtime. The jewel in the crown for this café, though, is the view from the tables, for the seating overlooks the Thames as it winds its way downstream and on a clear day Windsor Castle is visible. The view is fantastic and it is easy to see why it is among the most painted vistas in London.

The gardens are more formal than the Isabella Plantation. Part is dedicated to roses. Herbaceous borders and seasonal bedding plants are colourful in the summer, while in spring the laburnum arch is in full bloom. King Henry VIII's Mound is always worth a visit.

Originally, Pembroke Lodge was known as Molecatcher's Cottage. The molecatcher was employed to destroy molehills, making the way clear for huntsmen to gallop their horses freely over the land. (William III died of a fever that followed a fall while hunting when his horse stumbled on a molehill.)

Towards the end of the eighteenth century, Eliza, Countess of Pembroke, leased the property from the Crown – hence the present name. The original building was substantially altered and enlarged by the eminent architect Sir John Soane.

In 1847, Queen Victoria gave her then prime minister, Lord John Russell, the property for himself and his family. His grandson Bertrand Russell, the celebrated philosopher, pacifist and anti-nuclear campaigner, was born and brought up at the lodge.

During the Second World War the lodge was handed over to the Ministry of Defence for its Centre of Operations. Its crack 'Phantom' squadron was billeted here; one of their number was a Major David Niven, later to become a famous actor and author.

OPPOSITE, ABOVE: Pembroke Lodge.

OPPOSITE, BELOW: One of the more formal flower beds in the Pembroke Lodge garden.

BELOW: The laburnum arch.

Frogs congregate in the spring to
mate. It is important to leave the
spawn in the ponds undisturbed.

Reflections in the water of Leg of Mutton Pond.

ABOVE: Mallard with ducklings on
Adam's Pond.

OPPOSITE: Coot and chick on
Peg's Pond.

OVERLEAF: Swans on Adam's Pond.

OPPOSITE: The lower Pen Pond,
seen through trees.

BELOW, TOP: A reed bunting
perching on a bulrush.

BELOW, BOTTOM: Swans on
Adam's Pond.

Thatched House Lodge
and the nearby cottage.

summer

As the days grow longer and warmer, life in the park reaches its annual high point. Wild flowers now in full bloom attract bees, butterflies and other insects; birds and mammals are busy searching out food for their young.

By midsummer the woods have become quieter places. The vibrant bird song of spring has slackened but it has been replaced by the chirping of young fledglings eagerly awaiting their parents' return with food. The poor harassed things are trying desperately to assuage the insatiable appetites of their offspring.

As the days get longer, so the nights get shorter. This is the time to spot nocturnal species such as badgers, bats and owls as they emerge from their daytime resting places. With less time to forage in the darkness, they tend to come out at dusk.

This is also the time of year to see little owls. Their growing brood make staying in the nest a nightmare and they are often to be seen perching on trees and posts taking some respite from their demanding young. The fields behind Holly Lodge are a good place to spot them.

The grassland gradually changes from green to pale yellow and, walking through the grass, you see grasshoppers dancing about, disturbed momentarily. The stillness of a summer's evening amplifies their chirruping.

The deer are giving birth and the dappled young can be seen travelling among the rest of the herd.

Bats, attracted by the profusion of mosquitoes and midges, are visible flying backwards and forwards over the Pen Ponds, where wildfowl swim on the water, accompanied by their downy young, who are independent feeders from the time they hatch. Many ducks nest in trees and their young fall from the branches like laburnum seeds; after recovering from a heavy landing, they waddle to the nearest pond, where they remain until their flight feathers emerge. On the pond margins dragonflies and damselflies are visible.

butterflies and moths

A butterfly or moth begins life as an egg. The egg hatches into a caterpillar, which spends most of its life eating. When the caterpillar has absorbed the necessary amount of nutrients, it changes into a chrysalis or pupa. Inside the chrysalis, the cells become 'soup' and rearrange themselves into an adult. It is a process of complete metamorphosis.

Butterflies and moths usually spend a lot of time finding the right food plants on which to lay their eggs, so that the caterpillars will have a supply of food when they hatch. Butterflies, with their large often-colourful wings and antennae with well-defined knobs, fly by day, particularly in sunshine. Most moths fly at night or at dusk and are drab in colour. However, there are some day-flying moths, which have bright colourful wings. In flight the wings are similar in appearance to those of butterflies but when at rest they are mostly held down over the body, rather than vertically in the butterfly manner.

A butterfly that is often seen is the meadow brown, which is Britain's commonest butterfly. Meadow browns can be recognized by a false eye on a brown wing. They may be found all over the grassy meadows of the park.

The aristocrats – peacocks, red admirals and tortoiseshells – have beautiful wings. They love stinging nettles and are most likely to be found where there are nettles.

Cinnabar moths are common in the park. Their colours are red and black, warning birds that they are poisonous. They lay their eggs on groundsel leaves in June and July. They and their colourful yellow and black striped caterpillars can be easily spotted on the bright yellow groundsel plants.

The most common caterpillar to be seen in the park is that of the oak tortrix moth. These are the caterpillars that hang on long silky threads from oak trees and often attach themselves to you by accident as you walk in the woods. They feed on the oak leaves and if disturbed by predators they bale out and escape by hanging at the end of their thread. When the danger has passed, they climb back up their thread, gathering it as they go.

ABOVE: Rabbits emerge from their
burrow on a warm morning.

LEFT: Ragwort provides food for a
meadow brown butterfly.

the vista to St Paul's Cathedral

Shortly after St Paul's Cathedral, designed by Sir Christopher Wren, was completed in 1710, its medieval predecessor having been destroyed by the Great Fire in 1666, an avenue of trees was planted at Richmond Park. The avenue was aligned directly from King Henry VIII's Mound in the grounds of Pembroke Lodge towards England's grand new cathedral.

The mound is a prehistoric barrow or burial ground, situated at the park's highest point. It got its name from a fable that tells how Henry VIII sat on his horse on the mound watching for the cannon blast that was sounded after his second wife, Anne Boleyn, had been beheaded in the Tower of London. In fact historical evidence says that he was miles from Richmond at the time of her execution.

One hundred years after the original vista was devised, Sidmouth Wood was planted. To retain the view towards St Paul's a landscaped 'drift way' through the wood was created. During the 1940s, when many gardeners were away at war, the view vanished, obliterated by the growth of holly over the drift way as well as branches extending into the avenue through Sidmouth Wood.

In 1976, a local man, James Batten, rediscovered the vista and managed to restore it to its former glory. It is a magnificent sight on a clear day: a ten-mile pathway with only one building visible at the end – the dome of St Paul's Cathedral. This view currently enjoys statutory protection as one of the Strategic Views of St Paul's dome. The draft of the Mayor's Plan for London (2002) suggests that protection should be removed; however, this proposal has met with strong opposition.

The City of London skyline, seen from one of the highest points in the park, just below Richmond Gate.

OPPOSITE, ABOVE: A little owl looks down with a piercing stare from a dead tree trunk.

OPPOSITE, BELOW: A mackerel sky over the park.

BELOW: An incredible sky one evening over the copse near the Pen Ponds car park.

holly lodge

Holly Lodge is the administrative hub of the park. The Superintendent has his offices there, as does the Royal Parks Constabulary. Behind the original house, built in the mid-1830s, are new buildings housing the Holly Lodge Centre, the gamekeepers, and stables for the police horses and the shire horses that work in the park. The centre is a charitable establishment providing organized activities for schoolchildren from the surrounding area and students with special needs. It consists of a main classroom and the restored Victorian kitchen. The centre teaches history and natural history.

The kitchen is referred to as 'Mrs Sawyer's Kitchen', after the wife of Henry Sawyer, who was made Head Keeper of Richmond Park in 1872. He was the youngest man ever to hold the position. For the duration of his tenure he and his family lived at the lodge, which historically seems always to have been the home of the Head Keeper.

The office at the lodge offers information on things to see and do in the park. Postcards, the quarterly *Richmond Park Magazine* and pamphlets on the Isabella Plantation can be bought there.

Sunset, with the spire of St
Matthias's Church in Richmond
silhouetted against the sky.

Canada geese against the
evening sky.

dragonflies and damselflies

Along Beverley Brook and around the margins of the ponds in the park during the months of June, July and August dragonflies and damselflies can be spotted. Unlike butterflies and moths they do not go through four stages of metamorphosis, but have only three (this is called incomplete metamorphosis). They go from egg to nymph, then straight to adult. The eggs are laid on vegetation in water and hatch into nymphs. The nymph is a ferocious carnivorous predator and in some cases lives in the water for many years. The nymph transforms into the adult dragonfly, whose life is short, its only purpose being to mate and lay more eggs.

Dragonflies are of two types: hawkers and darters. The emperor dragonfly, the largest in the family, is a hawker and can be found tirelessly patrolling stretches of water at speeds of 18 miles an hour. It is very territorial, as are all dragonflies and damselflies. It usually lives for about one month after a nymphet stage lasting two years. Whereas hawkers are continually patrolling, darters are sturdier bodied and habitually spend time clinging to reeds and waterside vegetation. They make occasional raids and darts at prey or potential partners or intruders into their territory. Damselflies are more delicately built and smaller than dragonflies, and have a much weaker, dancing flight.

LEFT: A large red damselfly takes a rest on a marginal plant.

RIGHT: Buttercups among the drying grasses in Two Storm Wood.

ABOVE: A young kestrel surveys
its new territory.

LEFT: A little owlet emerges from
its nest, showing its amazing
camouflage.

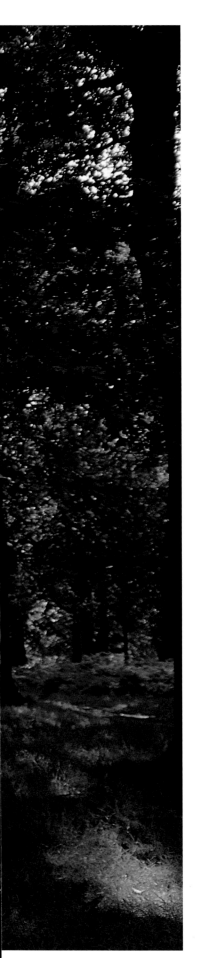

the mighty oak

Druids in Celtic Britian held the oak sacred and gathered miseltoe from its boughs for their secret rites. Then as now, the oak was the king of trees.

Richmond Park boasts many magnificent oak trees, some thought to be seven or even eight hundred years old. They were saplings long before the park was enclosed. An oak tree takes two hundred years to mature and it is said that one five-hundred-year-old oak tree is worth thousands of one-hundred-year-old oaks because of its increased biodiversity.

The longer a plant species has grown in a country, the more time insects have had to get used to feeding on it. After the last Ice Age oaks had already reappeared in Britain by 10,000 BC, and by 500 BC they were the dominant tree species. More insects are dependent on oaks than on any other British tree: 284 species of insects have been found living within their ecosystem. That number includes the caterpillars of 110 species of moths and butterflies, all eating the tender young first leaves (this compares to approximately five found on horse chestnut trees). Oak trees can survive complete defoliation by caterpillars in May. The sound of caterpillar droppings can be heard in woodlands like the patter of rain. The next shoots to arrive contain tannin, which caterpillars find unpalatable. By mid-August only sixty-five species of butterfly and moth remain. The top of the tree is inhabited by the purple hairstreak butterfly. Lower down is the oak tortrix moth. It is the caterpillars from this moth that are often found hanging from the trees on long silky threads.

The many insects present in an oak provide an immense amount of valuable food just when it is most needed by birds desperately trying to feed their hungry chicks.

Many birds use the oak as a nesting site. Crows have their nests near the top of the tree. Jackdaws and little owls use medium-sized holes, nuthatches and bluetits smaller ones. Woodpeckers make their own holes and starlings love old woodpecker nests. Tree creepers nest behind loose bark.

In the tree bark and wood you find beetles and bugs. Fungi decompose rotting wood, and beetle and fly larvae eat vegetation at the bottom of the tree and old fungi.

An oak wood is always a very open habitat. Shafts of sunlight on the woodland floor allow and encourage the growth of wild flowers such as bluebells.

The most famous tree in Richmond Park is probably seven hundred years old. Found at the southern end of Hornbeam Walk, it is known as John Martin's Oak after the artist who painted it 150 years ago. The picture is in the Victoria and Albert Museum.

Many of the oaks in the park have been pollarded. This is the technique of cutting the branches back to the trunk so that a thick head of branches is formed by the new growth. Especially in Tudor times, the cut wood was much used for furniture-making and ship-building. No doubt some of the wood from the park was used to make the ships that defeated the Spanish Armada.

Now oak trees that die or fall down are left to rot away naturally to encourage the wood-eating beetle larvae to stay.

Sunlight streams through the broadleaf woodland.

autumn

Autumn is the most eventful season in the park. September mornings start to get colder, and with the change in temperature come early morning mists. These hang low over the ground, the trees peering over the top hauntingly. Spiders' webs strung out on the grasses hang laden with dew, glinting as the low rays of the rising sun catch the droplets of water; the webs are always there but it is only now when the dew is on them that they become visible. It is necessary to get up early to experience these mists because they clear quite quickly once the sun hots up.

As September progresses the trees start to turn and the rut begins. At the height of the rut, the usually placid red deer stags maraud about at a gallop, ferns in their antlers, bellowing and grunting ferociously. Wet weather following a period of dry encourages fungi of all sorts, shapes and sizes to emerge.

By the end of November the rut is over, the leaves have fallen from the trees and the park returns to its relatively peaceful self.

ABOVE, LEFT: The old oak tree near Barn Wood, shown on pages 14–15 in winter mode, is seen here decked in autumn foliage.

ABOVE, RIGHT: A heron hunts in the corner of the pond near Conduit Wood. It is probably after unsuspecting frogs.

fungi

Fungi, the great rotters of the natural world, are at their most prolific in the autumn. It is said that without fungi, life would choke on its own waste and the soil lose its fertility. They can break down dead leaves, feathers and rotten wood, reducing them to humus and so returning nutrients to the soil.

The mushroom we see is only the reproductive part of the fungus, its fruiting body – the equivalent of an apple on a tree. The main part consists of thread-like hyphae, which penetrate the soil, dead leaves or living plants, absorbing nutrients. The hyphae spread out from each germinating spore, weaving together to form a mass called the mycelium.

Warm, damp weather and plentiful food provide the right conditions for the rapid growth needed for fungi to produce fruit bodies. Then the familiar mushrooms suddenly appear. For a few weeks they flourish, releasing millions of spores, until cold weather brings the season to an end. The mycelium beneath, however, can live for decades.

Although picking the mushrooms hardly affects the mycelium, harvesting them is forbidden in the park. This is because the mushrooms provide a valuable food source for many creatures that live there and action affecting one part of the food chain has repercussions all down the line.

ABOVE: A sulphur tuft or 'clustered wood lover' engulfing a tree stump.

LEFT: A close-up of the sulphur tuft.

LEFT: Delicate pink mushrooms emerge from a decaying tree.

RIGHT: 'Trumping crumble cap' or 'fairies' bonnets' mass on an oak tree.

the rut

The rut is an annual feature in the deer's life. It lasts about a month, starting in September, and it is when all next year's young are conceived.

By the end of the summer, the stags are reaching their peak condition. The deer mate in the autumn for births to take place in June and July. Wanting to mate with as many females as possible, a stag has to congregate a harem of females. He does this by aggressively herding in any female he sees. He collects together as many females as he can, but other males are always trying to steal them and on the outskirts of such harems hopeful adversaries strut their stuff.

Males prepare themselves for the rut by urinating in pools in which they then wallow, coating themselves with musky mud. They can be smelt at some distance if the wind is in the right direction.

Once a stag has a harem, he has to be constantly vigilant, making sure no rival impregnates one of his hinds. He has to stop the hinds from wandering off, fight off challengers and mate with the females. Needless to say there is not much time to sleep or eat. Stags lose an enormous amount of weight during the rut and are exhausted when it ends in October.

Very few fights occur. Most conflicts are decided by posturing – who bellows the loudest, who smells the strongest, who has the most vegetation on their antlers? Fights occur only when the males are very evenly matched. The two stags walk parallel to each other, bellowing and grunting, and then turn and clash antlers, pushing each other like two sumo wrestlers, seeing who is the strongest. They manoeuvre until one or other is dislodged and gives up. The victor chases off the loser.

The fallow deer stags have set territories which they mark by scraping hollows in the ground, scenting them with urine and rubbing the bark off saplings.

During rutting the stags are very edgy and it is dangerous to go too close – you may be seen as a rival. Usually the deer run away from people and dogs, but at this time of year, as in June when the young are born, they are not so timid.

BELOW, LEFT: A bellowing stag
during the rut.

BELOW, RIGHT: Two red deer stags
engage in battle during the rut.

ABOVE: Spiders' webs.

LEFT: The upper Pen Pond
shrouded in mist, the grasses
in the foreground covered with
spiders' webs.

leaf fall

bracken

Leaves use sunlight to make food for their plant. During the short days of winter, when there is less sunlight, trees cannot produce enough food to keep pace with the energy they use. As winter approaches, trees seal each leaf with a protective layer of cork at the base of the stalk. This is brittle, and when the branch is moved by the wind the leaves break off and flutter to the ground.

Before a tree sheds its leaves it extracts as much of their nutritious content as it can, starting with the chlorophyll, which gives the leaves their green colour, and then continuing with other pigments. As this happens, the leaves change from green through brown to the yellows and oranges made by pigments called carotenoids, which have accumulated in the leaves in the summer.

Bracken is a member of the fern family. Spores – the reproductive part of the plant – are found on the underside of the leaves, which are known as fronds. Bracken reproduces itself by dropping spores on the ground in wet weather. The spores have male and female reproductive cells and in the wet ground the male cells migrate to fertilize female cells. In the spring shoots emerge as tightly coiled buds. These grow rapidly, reaching a height of 6 feet/1.8 metres.

Bracken likes acid soil and it is very successful, spreading uncontrollably, because it is not palatable to grazing animals. Its fronds contain small quantities of cyanide.

In the park it needs to be contained because left unchecked it would infiltrate areas of precious acid grassland. Traditional methods of control are used to keep this invasive plant from spreading. The shire horses pull a bladed metal roller, which bends and crushes the fronds, over the bracken. Sap leaks out and the plants' vigour is reduced.

In the autumn, bracken is cut and collected and left in piles to rot down. In the early morning mist the piles steam and one of the finest sights of the autumn is of a deer staking its claim to one of these manmade mounds, the 'king of the castle' standing on top surveying his kingdom, his breath visible in the cold morning air.

In these mounds the decaying process starts. After a while the resulting compost is transferred to the Isabella Plantation, where the process continues until the acidic mulch is ready to be used to fertilize and improve the soil around the azaleas and rhododendrons.

ABOVE: Brilliant orange leaves nestle amongst moss-covered roots.

OPPOSITE: Startled red deer look on attentively.

ABOVE: Riders make the most of a beautiful morning.

RIGHT: Mute swans on the upper Pen Pond.

OVERLEAF: Sunset over Adam's Pond.

ABOVE: A squirrel forages for
acorns, before burying them
ready for winter.

LEFT: A majestic red deer stag
rests at the end of the rut.

our legacy

When Charles I created Richmond Park in 1637 by enclosing the area with a brick wall, he made himself very unpopular with the locals; but nearly four hundred years later all the people who enjoy the park are reaping the benefit of his arrogance, for it guaranteed that this vast and unique area was left untouched by development. There is no doubt that if the wall had not been erected Richmond Park would now be just another built-up area of houses and shops. Instead the enclosure of the park has allowed the ancient oaks and dry acid grasslands to provide a rich and varied habitat for many animals, birds and insects; and, in turn, people from an overcrowded city have a wonderful place to visit. English Nature designated Richmond Park a Site of Special Scientific Interest in 1992, and in 2000 the park was made a National Nature Reserve. This haven for wildlife and peaceful recreation, only ten miles from the heart of London, is one of the largest green areas in any city in the world.

ABOVE: The sun gets lower as winter draws nearer and the shadows lengthen.

LEFT: Beverley Brook in September.

Horse chestnut leaves fall and drift
on the still waters of Ham Pond.

After heavy rainfall, water cascades over the old tree stumps in the stream that runs through Conduit Wood.

index